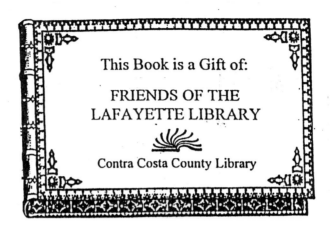

Watch It Grow

A Dog's Life

Nancy Dickmann

Heinemann Library
Chicago, Illinois

www.heinemannraintree.com
Visit our website to find out
more information about
Heinemann-Raintree books.

To order:

☎ Phone 888-454-2279

⌨ Visit www.heinemannraintree.com
to browse our catalog and order online.

Edited by Nancy Dickmann, Rebecca Rissman, and Catherine Veitch
Designed by Joanna Hinton-Malivoire
Picture research by Mica Brancic
Production by Victoria Fitzgerald
Originated by Capstone Global Library
Printed and bound in China by South China Printing Company Ltd

15 14 13 12 11 10
10 9 8 7 6 5 4 3 2 1

Library of Congress Cataloging-in-Publication Data
Dickmann, Nancy.
  A dog's life / Nancy Dickmann. -- 1st ed.
     p. cm. -- (Watch it grow)
  Includes bibliographical references and index.
  ISBN 978-1-4329-4229-8 (hc) -- ISBN 978-1-4329-4232-8 (pb) 1. Dogs--
Life cycles--Juvenile literature. I. Title.
  SF426.5.D53 2011
  636.7--dc22
                        2010000090

Acknowledgments
We would would like to thank the following for permission to reproduce
photographs: Alamy pp. **8** (© WoodyStock/Reichert Gabi), **9** (© Juniors
Bildarchiv/F240); Alamy [© Capstone Global Library Ltd] p. **13**
(© WoodyStock/Reichert Gabi [Tudor Photography]); © Capstone Global
Library Ltd pp. **7, 10, 11, 15, 16, 17, 18, 19 main, 20, 22 bottom,
22 left, 22 right, 22 top, 23 bottom, 23 middle, 23 top** (Tudor
Photography); iStockphoto pp. **4** (© Glen Jones), **14** (ronibgood56), **19
inset** (© Chris Bence); Nature Picture Library pp. **6** (© Lynn M. Stone), **12**
(© Adriano Bacchella); Photolibrary pp. **5** (Animals Animals/David Boyle),
21 (Picture Press/Joerg Lehmann).

Front cover photograph of beagle hound reproduced with permission
of Shutterstock (© Anke van Wyk). Inset photograph of a beagle puppy
reproduced with permission of iStockphoto (© Mariya Bibikova). Back cover
photograph of a mother beagle with puppies reproduced with permission
of Nature Picture Library (© Adriano Bacchella).

The publishers would like to thank Nancy Harris for her assistance in the
preparation of this book.

Every effort has been made to contact copyright holders of material
reproduced in this book. Any omissions will be rectified in subsequent
printings if notice is given to the publisher.

Contents

Life Cycles

All living things have a life cycle.

Dogs have a life cycle.

puppy

A puppy is born. It grows into a dog.

A female dog has puppies.
Later it will die.

Puppies

A female dog has puppies.

She licks the puppies.

The puppies cannot see or hear.

The puppies cannot walk.

mother

The puppies drink milk from their mother.

The puppies sleep together.

Growing Up

Soon the puppies open their eyes.

Soon the puppies learn to walk.

The puppies play together.

puppy food

The puppies start to eat puppy food.

Becoming a Dog

A puppy grows into a dog.

dog biscuits

A dog eats meat and dog biscuits.

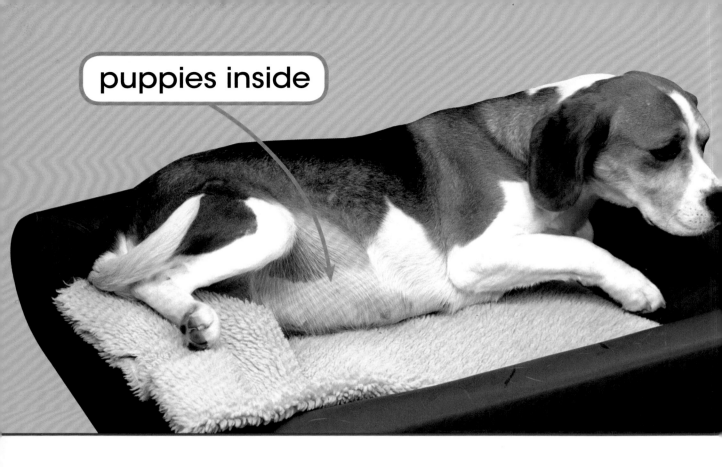

A female dog is ready to
have puppies.

The life cycle starts again.

Life Cycle of a Dog

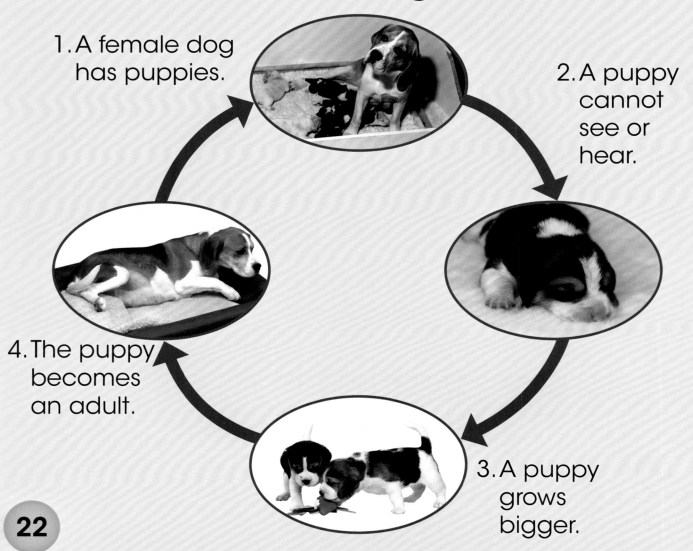

1. A female dog has puppies.

2. A puppy cannot see or hear.

3. A puppy grows bigger.

4. The puppy becomes an adult.

22

Picture Glossary

female able to have babies. A girl is a female.

meat food that comes from the bodies of animals. Dogs eat meat.

puppy a young dog

Index

Notes to Parents and Teachers
Before reading
Ask the children if they know what a baby dog is called. Then see if they can name a baby cat, horse, cow, sheep, and pig. Talk about how some babies look like small versions of the adults. Can they think of any other baby animals that look like the adults?

After reading
- Take the children to an animal shelter to see some newly born puppies and their mother. Get the children to take photos of the puppies and dog or to draw them. Back in the classroom, make a list of things they noticed about the puppies. Did the puppies have their eyes closed? What did they eat and drink? Were they walking? Were the puppies the same color as their mother?
- Help children to make their own animal matching game. Give children a selection of photos of adult animals and baby animals. Include some baby animals that don't look like the adults. Ask the children to cut out the photos and stick them on pieces of construction paper or index cards. Then have the children try to match up each adult with its baby. They can also play a memory game to find the pairs of cards that go together.